Weatherworks

BY JERI CIPRIANO

Table of Contents

1. Weather Watch 2

2. Experiments with Heat 4

3. Experiments with Air and Wind 10

4. Experiments with Water 20

5. Charting the Weather 30

Glossary 31

Index 32

CHAPTER 1

Weather Watch

How is the **weather** today where you live? Is it a bright, clear day? Or is it dark and cloudy? Weather is the daily condition of the **air** around you. It can be hot or cold, wet or dry, sunny or cloudy, windy or calm.

People have always wondered about the weather. Why does it rain? Why do **winds** blow? What causes thunder and **lightning**? Why do we see a rainbow after it rains?

The factors that are most important in weather are the sun, air, and water. The way these three factors interact determines what the weather will be. The experiments in this book will help you understand these factors. They will also give you a better understanding of weather in general.

Not Too Hot or Too Cold

Temperatures on Earth are not the same all over. They range from a low of -76° Fahrenheit to a high well over 100° Fahrenheit (-60° to 37.7° Celsius). Temperatures vary because all parts of Earth do not receive the same amount of heat energy from the sun. Differences in the temperature of the air cause differences in weather conditions.

The sun's energy warms Earth. The **atmosphere**, a thick layer of gases, absorbs and stores this energy. The atmosphere also protects Earth from the harmful effects of the sun's radiation.

Think it over!

Farmers, sailors, and pilots watch the weather very carefully. Can you guess why? Can you think of anyone else who might need to watch the weather carefully? Write down your ideas.

Experiments with Heat

The sun is a star, a ball of hot glowing gases that releases huge amounts of heat, light, and other forms of energy into space. Only a small amount of the sun's energy reaches Earth, but it is enough to light and warm the entire planet.

Sunny Side Up

Why is it hotter in the summer than in the winter? One reason is that there are more hours of sunlight on summer days than on winter days. But the main reason has to do with the angle at which the sun's rays strike Earth.

At the equator, it is warm all the time. The sun's rays strike Earth at a 90° angle all year long. When the sun's rays are perpendicular to Earth (90° angle), they are most direct.

In the Northern Hemisphere, it is warmer in the summer and colder in the winter. This is because in the summer, the sun's rays strike the Northern Hemisphere directly. In the winter, the sun's rays strike the Northern Hemisphere at an angle. When the sun's rays strike Earth directly, the greatest amount of heating occurs. When the rays strike Earth at an angle, less of the sun's energy is received by Earth. As the angle of the rays becomes smaller, the rays become less direct. The same amount of energy is spread over a wider area.

To see how this works, try the following experiment.

What you need:

- a table lamp

What to do:

1. Palm side down, put your hand directly under the bulb of the lamp at a distance of about three inches. Be careful not to get too close to the hot bulb. How does your hand feel?

2. Move your hand to the right about five inches. Is there any change? Move your hand to the left about five inches. What happens?

Weather Report

Your hand feels cooler five inches to the right or left of the bulb because the rays from the lamp are striking your hand at an angle. This is the way the sun's rays strike Earth during the winter. When the rays from the lamp are traveling straight down to your hand, they are like the sun's direct rays in the summer.

A Day at the Beach

The sun heats the entire Earth—the land, oceans, and air. But these three materials do not all heat up at the same rate. Water takes longer to heat up than land and air. But water loses its heat more slowly than land and air. This means water stays warmer longer.

Try this experiment to prove that land, water, and air heat up and lose their heat at different rates. You will do this by comparing their temperatures under different conditions.

What you need:

- **3 plastic cups**
- **1 cup of sand**
- **1 cup of water**
- **3 outdoor thermometers**

What to do:

1. Put water in one cup and sand in another. Keep the third cup empty.

2. Place a thermometer in each cup.

3. After a few minutes, record the temperature reading of each thermometer.

4. Put all three cups on a sunny windowsill for 30 minutes.

5. Record the temperature reading of each thermometer. Which cup or cups have the highest temperature?

6. Place all three cups in the refrigerator for 15 minutes.

7. Remove the cups from the refrigerator and record the temperature reading of each thermometer. Which cup has the highest temperature? Which cup has the lowest temperature?

Weather Report

On the windowsill, the sand and the air got warm while the water remained cooler. That's because the sand and the air heated up faster than the water. Sand keeps the heat near the surface. If you dig in the sand on a hot day, you'll find that the sand underneath is still cool. When the sun goes down, the sand gives up its heat quickly, but the temperature of the water remains more constant.

Watch your thermometer and see how temperatures change throughout the day.

What happens if the thermometer is in shade? In sunlight? How does wind affect the thermometer?

Ups and Downs

The temperature of the air is measured with a thermometer. Most thermometers consist of a thin glass tube with a bulb at one end. The bulb is filled with a liquid that is colored with dye. Along the side of the glass tube is a scale marked off in degrees, which is the unit used to measure temperature.

In the United States, the temperature scale used is called the Fahrenheit scale (F). Scientists and people in other countries use a scale called Celsius, or centigrade (C). When it's 80° F (26.6° C), you know to put on lightweight clothes. When it's 5° F (-15° C), it means you should wear your winter coat.

Try this experiment to find out how a thermometer works.

What you need:

- five ice cubes
- cup of water
- outdoor thermometer

What to do:

1. Put five ice cubes into a cup of water.

2. Look at the thermometer. At what number is the thin red line?

3. Place the thermometer in the ice water. Watch the thin red line move. What do you notice is happening to the thin red line?

4. Remove the thermometer.

5. Put your thumb over the red bulb at the bottom of the thermometer. What do you notice is happening to the thin red line?

Weather Report

As the red liquid cools, the molecules move closer together (contract). The red liquid takes up less space so the red line moves down.

As the red liquid heats up, the molecules move farther apart (expand). The red liquid takes up more space so the red line moves up.

9

Experiments with Air and Wind

Amazing Air

Every second of every day, you have a great weight pushing on you. It's called air! Although air particles are invisible, they still have weight. The force exerted on you by the weight of the tiny air particles is called **air pressure**.

Air is a gas. You can't see it. You can't smell it. You can't taste it. Yet air has weight, and you can prove it with this experiment!

What you need:

- **clothes hanger**
- **2 twist-ties**
- **2 small kitchen garbage bags**
- **scissors**

What to do:

1. Using your finger, hold the hanger under its hook. The hanger should balance. Both corners of the hanger should be even.

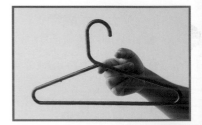

2. Fill up one garbage bag with air. One way to do this is to place the bag in front of a small fan. Or you might blow into the bag several times. Tie the bag up quickly so the air does not escape.

3. The other bag should be empty. To get out as much air as possible, put the bag on a flat surface and use your hand to flatten it. Tie the bag up quickly.

4. Tie each bag to one of the lower corners of the hanger.

5. Balance the hook of the hanger on your finger again. What do you notice? What does this tell you about the bag filled with air compared to the empty bag?

It's a FACT

Hold out your hand, palm upward. You are holding an invisible weight. This weight is the air pressing down on your hand.

Weather Report

The air-filled bag pulls down its corner of the hanger because of the weight of the added air. The air-filled bag is heavier than the empty bag.

Need a Lift?

Earth's atmosphere is so heavy that at sea level it presses down on you with a force of 14.7 pounds per square inch! You are made up of a lot of square inches! So why doesn't the air crush you? The answer is that the air and other fluids inside your body exert pressure, too. That pressure balances the pressure of the air outside.

Air pressure measures the force of air. How strong is this force? Can it hold up a glass of water? Try this experiment to find out.

What you need:

- plastic drinking glass
- square of thick cardboard (larger than the glass opening)
- bowl or a sink

What to do:

1. Fill a plastic glass with water all the way to the top.

2. Press a square of cardboard on top to make a tight seal.

3. (Do this step over a bowl or a sink.) Holding the cardboard in place, very carefully turn the glass over. Then remove your hand from the cardboard and continue to hold the glass at the top. Does the water stay in the glass?

Weather Report

Air presses in all directions. It pushes upward on the cardboard with enough pressure to hold the water in place. The pressure pushing up on the cardboard is greater than the pressure pushing down.

WHY DO MY EARS "POP"?

Air is made up of particles called molecules. When the molecules are close together, or compressed, the air exerts a greater pressure. When there is more space between the molecules, the air exerts less pressure.

When you're in an airplane or on top of a mountain, there are fewer air molecules so the air pressure is less. But the pressure inside your body does not change. The pressure inside and outside your ears is not equal. To balance the pressure, air rushes out of your ears and they "pop."

An "Air-Raising" Feat!

You now know that air and other gases have weight and exert pressure. This experiment will demonstrate that gases, like all matter, take up space. The gas produced in this experiment is carbon dioxide. It forms when vinegar and baking soda are combined.

What you need:

- funnel
- balloon
- vinegar
- baking soda
- plastic soda or water bottle

What to do:

1. Using the funnel to avoid spills, pour enough vinegar into the bottle to make it about half full.

2. Place the funnel in the neck of the balloon and sprinkle some baking soda into the balloon.

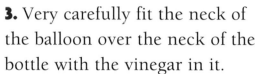

3. Very carefully fit the neck of the balloon over the neck of the bottle with the vinegar in it.

4. Slowly lift up the balloon so that the baking soda falls into the vinegar. What happens to the balloon as the mixture starts to fizz?

Weather Report

When the baking soda mixes with the vinegar, a reaction takes place. A gas is produced. The gas fills the balloon, causing it to expand.

Air on the Move

Wind is air in motion. Air pressure and temperature determine whether we can expect a gentle breeze or gale-force winds. Without wind, there would be few changes in our weather.

Winds are named by the direction from which they come, not toward which they blow. For example, if you feel a wind in your face while facing east, it is an east wind.

When measuring wind, we describe its speed and direction. Wind direction is determined using a weather vane. Explore wind direction by making your own weather vane.

What you need:

- flowerpot (4" diameter)
- compass
- soil or sand
- pencil with an eraser
- scissors
- tape
- two, colored index cards
- drinking straw
- marker
- straight pin

What to do:

1. Fill the flowerpot with soil or sand.

2. Cut out a square from one index card that will fit inside the flowerpot and cover most of the soil or sand. Mark each corner with the points of a compass—**N**(orth), **S**(outh), **E**(ast), **W**(est).

3. Fold the square in half and snip a small hole in the center. Open the square and place it over the filled flowerpot. Then carefully push the sharp end of the pencil through the center hole and into the soil or sand.

4. Cut out a triangle from the other index card. Tape it to one end of the straw to make an arrow. Then cut out a rectangle that is somewhat larger than the arrow. Tape it to the other end of the straw.

5. Push the straight pin through the middle of the straw. Then insert the tip of the pin into the eraser end of the pencil. Make sure the pin can turn easily.

6. Place your weather vane outside. Use the compass to position it correctly. The **N** on your weather vane should be facing north, as indicated by the compass.

Weather Report

People say that east winds often bring rain, and west winds indicate clearing. North winds often forecast cold weather, and south winds bring warm weather. What does your weather vane forecast? Remember that the arrow on your weather vane points into the wind, which means in the direction from which the wind is blowing.

17

Twister!

Tornadoes—you've seen them on television, in the movies, and perhaps even in real life. What is a tornado? A tornado is a violent, whirling column of wind spiraling around a center of low atmospheric pressure. Appearing as a dark, funnel-shaped cloud, a tornado travels very quickly, destroying everything in its path.

In this experiment, you will use water to create a tornado in a bottle.

What you need:

- funnel
- 2 empty, plastic soda bottles, labels removed
- pitcher of water
- heavy duct tape

It's a FACT

The word "tornado" comes from the Latin *tonare*, meaning "to thunder." The Spanish developed the word into *tornear*, "to turn or twist."

18

What to do:

1. Using the funnel, pour water into one bottle until it is about three-quarters full.

2. Hold the empty bottle upside down and position the opening over the opening of the filled bottle. Tape the two bottles together at the necks with duct tape. You will need to wind the duct tape around several times to be sure the bottles are secure and won't leak.

3. Turn the bottles upside down so the full bottle is now on top. Hold the bottom bottle as you swirl the bottles in a circular motion.

Weather Report

The swirling motion will create a **vortex**, a rotating column of water. A real tornado is a vortex of air. Your tornado is a vortex of water.

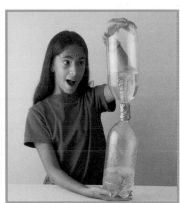

Experiments with Water

Making Clouds

When you look up in the sky, one of the most obvious things you see is **clouds**. Clouds form as a result of **condensation**. Moisture in the air condenses, or changes from a gas to a liquid, on small particles of dust or other solids. The moisture condenses because the air cools. Clouds play a key role in determining the weather. Not only are clouds the source of rain and snow, but they also affect the temperature. Clouds block the sun's rays, keeping Earth cool.

Experiment with clouds by making your very own.

What you need:
- **ice cubes**
- **warm water**
- **metal pan**
- **plastic jar**

What to do:

1. Put some ice cubes in a metal pan until the pan becomes very cold.

2. Pour an inch or two of warm water into the jar.

3. Place the cold metal pan with ice cubes over the top of the jar. Watch what happens.

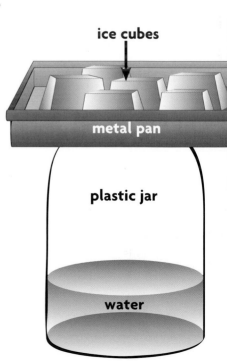

ice cubes

metal pan

plastic jar

water

CLOUD CLASSIFICATION

Clouds come in lots of different shapes and sizes. To identify different clouds, scientists created a classification system that divides clouds into five groups based on their shape, structure, and height above the ground.

cirrus

altostratus

cumulus

cumulonimbus

stratus

Weather Report

Water vapor is the gas form of water. Like most gases, it is invisible. Water vapor rises out of the warm water in the jar. When it is cooled by the cold pan, it condenses, or turns back into small floating droplets of water. These droplets are seen as clouds, mist, or fog.

Rain Maker

Clouds are made up of tiny water droplets and/or ice crystals that have condensed around particles of dust. These droplets and crystals are not yet heavy enough to fall to the ground as rain or snow. So how do rain and snow happen?

Cloud droplets must increase in size before rain or snow falls. They do this by colliding and combining with other droplets. At some point, the droplets get too large to remain suspended in the cloud. Gravity pulls them to Earth.

Rain and snow come down from the clouds and fall into oceans, rivers, lakes, and ponds on Earth. At the same time, water from oceans, rivers, lakes, and ponds **evaporates** into the air. The water vapor forms clouds and the process continues over and over again. It is called the water cycle.

This experiment gives you a chance to make your own rain and observe the water cycle.

The water cycle replenishes Earth's supply of water. ↓

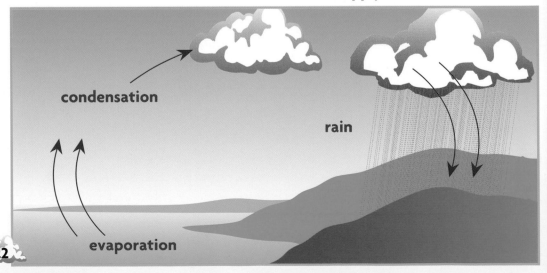

condensation

rain

evaporation

What you need:

- **adult helper**
- **small pot**
- **water**
- **5–6 ice cubes**
- **metal pie pan**
- **pot holder**
- **stove**

What to do:

1. Have an adult fill a pot half-full with water and bring it to a boil on the stove. When the water boils, a cloud of condensed steam will form.

2. Put the ice cubes in the pie pan and have the adult hold the pan over the pot. Look at the bottom of the pan. What's happening?

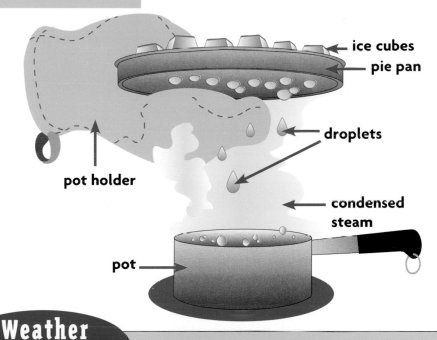

ice cubes

pie pan

droplets

pot holder

condensed steam

pot

Weather Report   Water droplets form on the bottom of the pie pan. Those droplets are just like rain. The water at the bottom of the pan came from the "cloud" over the pot.

It's a FACT

Water evaporates from your body, too. It's called sweat. On days when there is a lot of water vapor in the air (high-humidity days), your sweat evaporates slowly. This is because the air already contains a lot of moisture. On low-humidity days, sweat evaporates quickly, cooling you and leaving you feeling dry.

Rain, Rain, Go Away

What happens to puddles of rain after a storm? They disappear as a result of evaporation. Evaporation takes place when the sun's heat changes rainwater into invisible water vapor. The water appears to have "dried up." The amount of water vapor in the air is called **humidity**. You can see how evaporation happens in this experiment.

What you need:
- **two saucers the same size**
- **cold water**
- **sunny windowsill**
- **hardcover book**

What to do:

Put two saucers on a sunny windowsill. Add the same amount of cold water to each. Block the sun's rays from one saucer with an open book. Wait a while. What happens?

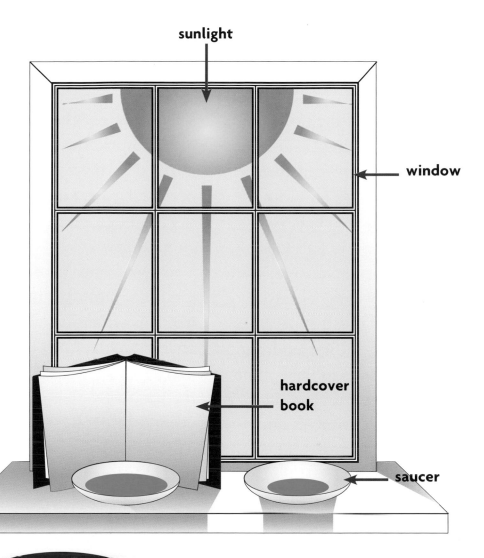

sunlight

window

hardcover book

saucer

Weather Report

The water in the saucer that is in direct sunlight evaporates more quickly than the water in the saucer that is shaded from the sun.

Sound and Light Show

What creates the brilliant flashes of lightning that often accompany heavy rainstorms? Electrical charges build up inside clouds. It is believed that smaller cloud particles develop a positive charge, while larger ones become negatively charged. The positive particles go to the top of the cloud, the negative particles to the bottom. The attraction between the charges grows stronger and eventually overcomes the air's resistance to electrical flow.

The negatively charged particles move toward the positively charged particles, and lightning occurs. This is known as cloud-to-cloud lightning—the most common type.

There is also cloud-to-ground lightning. This happens when the negatively charged particles in the lower part of a cloud are attracted to the positively charged ground below.

How can you make lightning? Read on to find out.

It's a FACT

• The electricity formed by lightning is brighter than 10 million 100-watt light bulbs, and travels at a speed of 60 miles per second.

• Lightning and thunder happen at the same time, but light travels faster than sound. If you count the seconds between the flash of lightning and the clap of thunder, then divide by 5 (for miles) or by 3 (for kilometers), you'll know how far away the storm is.

What you need:

- **hair comb**
- **piece of wool**
- **metal doorknob**

What to do:

1. Turn out the lights so the room is as dark as you can make it.

2. Rub the comb with the piece of wool a few times.

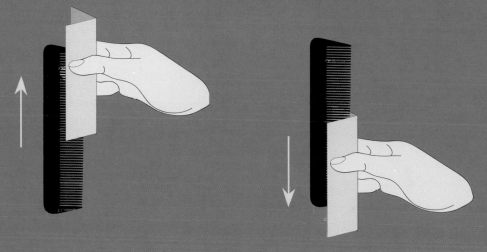

3. Touch the comb to the metal doorknob. See what happens.

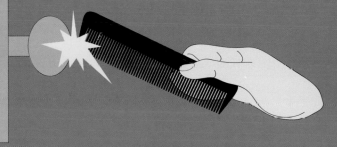

Weather Report

When you rub the comb with the wool, you give it a charge. When the charge jumps to the metal doorknob, a "spark" results. Lightning is the spark that results from charges jumping from one cloud to another or to the ground.

27

→   →   →   →   →   →   →

It's a FACT

What you need:

- sunny day
- garden hose

A Most Colorful Ending

Why do we see a rainbow after it rains? Rainbows form when light, water, and air meet in the sky. They occur during or just after it rains, while the sun is shining and the air contains raindrops. When the sun's rays pass through the raindrops, we see all the colors of the **spectrum**. Although light appears to be white, it is really made up of red, orange, yellow, green, blue, indigo, and violet.

In this final experiment, you can make a rainbow with a garden hose.

What to do:

Stand with your back to the sun. Create a spray of mist with the garden hose. What do you see? A rainbow will appear in the mist.

Weather Report

In the sky, rainbows are curved because of the way sunlight hits round raindrops. The arc you see from the ground is just a part of a rainbow. Rainbows are, in fact, circles. Only a person flying in a plane can see a rainbow's complete circle.

CHAPTER 5

Charting the Weather

Now that you've learned more about the weather, you can compare your local weather to weather in other places around the country. Using a chart like the one below, track the weather in your area and in two cities from other regions of the United States.

You can get current weather information from several sources, including newspapers, national news reports, and Web sites. The Internet Weather Source at http://weather.noaa.gov and The Weather Channel at www.weather.com are two good sites.

	HOMETOWN	CITY 1	CITY 2
Date			
Time			
Temperature			
Humidity			
Wind speed			
Wind direction			
Air pressure			
Precipitation			

Glossary

air	(AIR) a mixture of gases that makes up the atmosphere
air pressure	(AIR PREH-sher) the weight of air pressing down on Earth
atmosphere	(AT-muh-sfeer) layers of air that surround Earth, which are thickest nearest the ground and fade away to nothing in space
cloud	(KLOWD) a mass of water droplets that floats in the air
condensation	(kahn-den-SAY-shun) the change from gas to liquid
evaporates	(ih-VA-puh-rates) changes from liquid to gas
humidity	(hyoo-MIH-dih-tee) the amount of moisture or water vapor in the air
lightning	(LITE-ning) a strong flash of electricity between two clouds or a cloud and the ground
spectrum	(SPEK-trum) the spread of colors found in light in the order of red, orange, yellow, green, blue, indigo, and violet
temperature	(TEM-puh-ruh-cher) a measure of hotness and coldness
vortex	(VOR-teks) a rotating column of water or air
water vapor	(WAU-ter VAY-per) water that is held in the air in the form of gas
weather	(WEH-ther) all the changing conditions of temperature, wind, and moisture
wind	(WIND) air moving over the ground

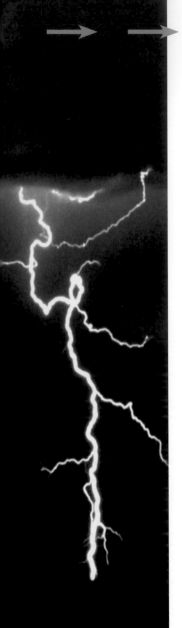

Index

air, 2, 6, 10–17, 19–20, 22, 24, 26, 28

air pressure, 10–14, 30

atmosphere, 2, 12

cloud, 20–23

condensation, 20–22

evaporation, 22, 24–25

fog, 21

humidity, 24, 30

lightning, 2, 26–27

mist, 21

molecules, 9, 13

rain, 2, 20, 22, 24, 28

rainbow, 2, 28–29

snow, 22

spectrum, 28

summer, 4–5

sun, 2, 4–7

temperature, 2, 6–9, 30

thermometer, 6–9

thunder, 2, 26

tornado, 18–19

vortex, 19

water vapor, 21–24

weather, 2–3, 5, 7, 9, 11, 13, 15–17, 19, 21, 23, 25,27, 29–30

weather vane, 16–17

wind, 2, 16–17